anythink

D0602439

EVERYDAY HISTORY

LIFE IN

ROMAN TIMES

SARAH RIDLEY

A⁺

Smart Apple Media

Published by Smart Apple Media, an imprint of Black Rabbit Books
P.O. Box 3263, Mankato, Minnesota 56002
www.smartapplemedia.com

Published by arrangement with Watts Publishing, London.

Library of Congress Cataloging-in-Publication Data
Ridley, Sarah, 1963-
  Life in Roman times / Sarah Ridley.
      pages cm. — (Everyday history)
  Includes index.
   ISBN 978-1-59920-951-7
  eISBN 978-1-68071-006-9
1. Rome—Civilization—Juvenile literature. I. Title.
  DG77.R55 2015
  937—dc23
                                 2013033419

Picture credits:
Ancient Art and Architecture Collection: 7b, 18t, 20t, 25b.
Courtesy of the Trustees of the British Museum: front cover br, 7t, 8t, 10t, 22t, 26t.
Colchester Museums: 24t.
Mike Corbishley: 6t.
Michael Holford: front cover bl, 6c, 16t (both), 28t.
Museum of London: front cover tr, 6b.
Vinolanda Trust 14t.
Roger White: 12t.
Reproduced by Courtesy of the Yorkshire Museum/Woodmansterne: 5t, 30t.

Printed in the United States by CG Book Printers
North Mankato, Minnesota

PO 1729
3-2015

CONTENTS

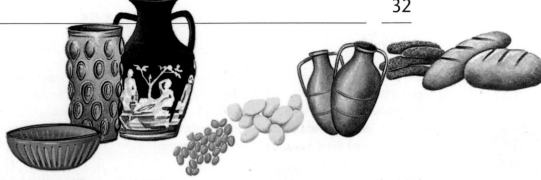

WHO WERE THE ROMANS?

Two thousand years ago, the Romans were the most powerful nation in Europe and around the Mediterranean Sea. About 60 million people lived in their empire. The official language of all these people was Latin but they spoke their own languages as well — such as Celtic and ancient Greek.

The Roman Empire began when the tribe known as the *Latins* took over the city of Rome in Italy. They began to conquer the lands around them and became known as the Romans. Wherever they went, they built towns and introduced Roman life.

Roman coins

This map (*right*) shows the Roman Empire about 1,800 years ago.

BRITANNIA

BELGICA

LUGDUNENSIS
GALLIA

AQUITANIA

ATLANTIC OCEAN

NARBONENSIS

TARRACONENSIS

LUSITANIA

BAETICA

MAURETANIA
CEASARIENSIS

MAURETANIA
TINGITANA

SOME IMPORTANT DATES FROM ROMAN TIMES

800–400 BC

753 Legend says Rome was founded by Romulus.

400–100 BC

264–241 First Punic War against the Carthaginians.
218–201 Second Punic War. Hannibal crosses the Alps by elephant to attack the Romans.
149–146 Final Punic War — Carthaginians defeated.

100 BC–0 AD

58–49 Julius Caesar conquers Gaul (France) and invades Britain.
27 Augustus becomes Rome's first emperor.

AD 1–100

14 Emperor Augustus dies.
43 The Romans conquer Britain.
79 Mount Vesuvius in Italy erupts and the cities of Pompeii and Herculaneum are destroyed.

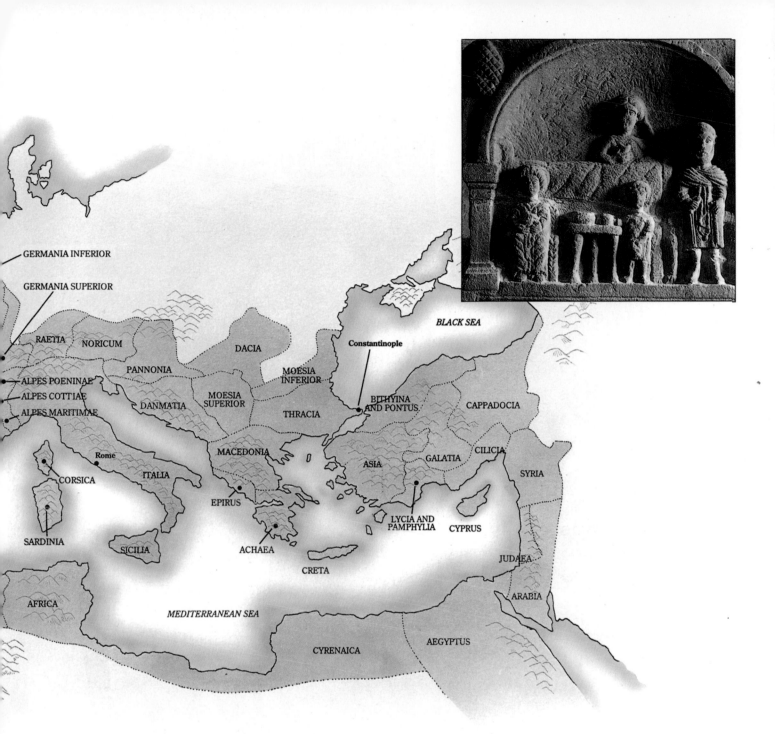

GERMANIA INFERIOR

GERMANIA SUPERIOR

RAETIA NORICUM

ALPES POENINAE

ALPES COTTIAE

ALPES MARITIMAE

PANNONIA

DANMATIA

CORSICA

ITALIA

Rome

SARDINIA

SICILIA

AFRICA

MEDITERRANEAN SEA

DACIA

MOESIA
SUPERIOR

MOESIA
INFERIOR

THRACIA

MACEDONIA

EPIRUS

ACHAEA

CRETA

CYRENAICA

BLACK SEA

Constantinople

BITHYINA
AND PONTUS

ASIA

GALATIA

CAPPADOCIA

CILICIA

LYCIA AND
PAMPHYLIA

CYPRUS

SYRIA

JUDAEA

ARABIA

AEGYPTUS

AD 100–200

122 Emperor Hadrian rules. Hadrian's Wall is begun in northern Britain.

AD 200–300

212 All free men are made Roman citizens.
284 The Roman Empire is divided into two parts—east and west.

AD 300–400

312 Emperor Constantine rules. He chose Byzantium as the new capital city in the east and named it Constantinople.
367 Britain is attacked by "barbarians."

AD 400–600

409 German armies attack Rome.
476 The last Roman emperor is overthrown and the western empire collapses.

HOW DO WE KNOW ABOUT THE ROMANS?

Detectives look for clues to help them solve crimes. Archaeologists and historians call their clues to the past "evidence." We can find out about the Romans from three sorts of evidence—the clues discovered by archaeologists, buildings that are still standing today and Roman writings.

ARCHAEOLOGICAL EVIDENCE

What do you think happens to the things you throw away? When your trash can is emptied, paper and foods rot away. Materials such as fabric and wood take longer. Materials such as glass and some metals never rot. In the same way, only some objects survive from Roman times. Many of these objects were found in Roman garbage pits, settlement sites, or graves. Archaeologists have to decide what all of this evidence means and what it tells them about Roman times.

Archaeologists carefully excavate a Roman site (above). This Roman mosaic (below) gives us information about how the Romans harvested grapes and made wine.

These Roman shoes have survived because the leather they are made from has been preserved in wet ground.

ROMAN WRITING

The Romans left us accounts of their wars, plays, poems, recipe books, and letters, among other writings. Only rarely do the original pieces of writing survive. However, we can still read Roman writings because many of them were copied out by monks in the medieval period.

The letter above has survived from Roman times. It was found at Hadrian's Wall and is a birthday party invitation. It was written on a very thin piece of wood (see page 20 for more on Roman writing materials).

STANDING STRUCTURES

In many places, Roman buildings have survived. Sometimes we can see the remains of whole towns, such as Pompeii, Italy. This city was buried under volcanic ash in AD 79.

This building is the Colosseum in Rome, a huge amphitheater built for gladiator fights and spectacular shows.

ON THE FARM

Most people in the Roman Empire lived in the countryside and farmed the land. At harvest time, workers cut the grain crops using sickles like this one (*right*). One part of this sickle is missing—the wooden handle. The metal blade has rusted over time.

This sickle's edge was kept very sharp with a sharpening stone called a whetstone.

FARMING

Many of the people who worked on the land were slaves—people taken prisoner in wars across the empire. They became the property of landowners with huge farm estates. These estates needed vast numbers of workers to grow crops and look after animals. However, not all the farms in the Roman Empire were large estates. Small farms, especially in Italy, were owned by one family with the help of only one or two slaves.

MYSTERY OBJECT

If you lived in Roman times, you might have seen this clever piece of equipment on a farm. What is it? (Answer on page 32.)

Farmworkers grab a handful of corn and slice through the stalks with the sickle.

SOME OF THE CROPS GROWN BY THE ROMANS

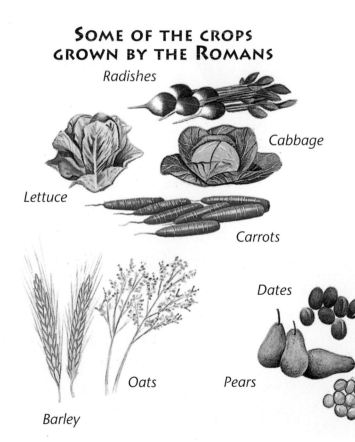

Radishes

Cabbage

Lettuce

Carrots

Oats

Barley

Dates

Pears

Apples

Cherries

Grapes

ON THE FARM

A big farm was called a *villa*. The Romans also used the word for a country or seaside house. Wealthy Romans owned one or more villas, and a town or city home where they lived most of the year. When the landowner was away, a farm manager ran the farm. He grew a mixture of crops (*left*), or concentrated on just one crop, like grapes to make wine.

IN THE KITCHEN

Only wealthy Romans had proper kitchens at home. The cook used this *mortarium*, which we call a mortar (the bowl) and pestle (the grinder). It was like a food processor and was used to grind up spices and mix up sauces by hand.

EATING OUT

In towns and cities, many people cooked over a brazier, a basic grill, or had no kitchen at all. They bought hot food from street bars, and bread, olives, fruit, and cheese from shops and stalls.

These are some of the items for sale in shops and bars.

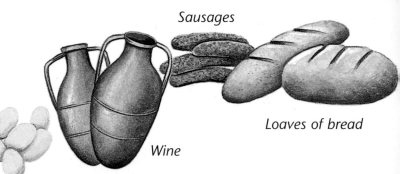

Sausages

Loaves of bread

Wine

Eggs

Olives

Bars, like the one shown here, sold a variety of snacks as well as drinks, such as watered-down wine and honey water. Tables and benches were provided to eat at inside, or you could stand at the bar. How much fish or meat people ate depended on their wealth.

Slaves did all the cooking in most wealthy homes.

MAKE YOUR OWN SWEETS

Here are two recipes from the Roman cookery writer, Apicius.

STUFFED DATES:

Remove the stones and fill the dates with nuts, pine kernels, or pepper. Roll in salt and fry in honey.

HONEYED BREAD:

Soak pieces of bread in milk and then fry in olive oil. Pour honey on the bread before serving.

IN THE KITCHEN

Most food was cooked in pots over a charcoal fire. The cook prepared the main meal of the day in the afternoon. Wealthy Romans often asked friends to join them for dinner. This kept the cook busy producing fish and meat dishes and strong-tasting sauces.

SOMEWHERE TO LIVE

Wealthy Romans filled their homes with comfortable furniture like this couch. Only the wooden frame survives today, but historians have added material to show its full shape. It would have had a padded back, arms, and seat like the one on the next page.

APARTMENT OR HOUSE?

Where people lived depended on whether they were rich or poor. In towns and cities, most people lived in apartments while the poorest people lived in one-room homes. More wealthy people could afford a large apartment or a townhouse and maybe a country house on the farm.

IN THE GARDEN

Larger houses were built around a square courtyard open to the sky. Many had carefully laid out gardens. The family walked along paths shaded by plants and trees and lined with flowers and herbs.

Grapevines

Bay tree

Fig tree

Parsley

Fennel

Mint

Apple tree

Cherry tree

A wealthy lady sits on her comfortable couch in the living room.

WALLS AND FLOORS

Wealthy Romans liked well-decorated homes. They paid artists to paint pictures (murals) on the walls and hung up painted wooden panels. Mosaic floors were popular. Craftsmen created pictures or patterns using thousands of colored tiles stuck to the floor with plaster.

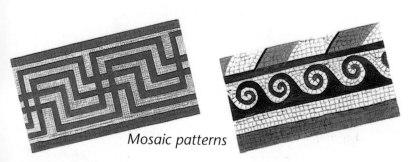

Mosaic patterns

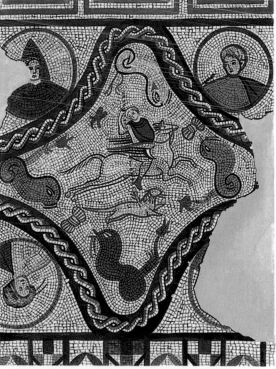

A drawing of a Roman mosaic found in Lullingstone, England.

13

WHAT SHALL I WEAR TODAY?

Women wore sandals like this on special occasions, or when they had guests. This leather sandal was made for a wealthy Roman lady who lived in Britain. We even know the name of the shoemaker, L. AEB. THALES T.F. (Lucius Aebutius Thales, son of Titus), which is stamped on the sole.

CLOTHES FOR ALL

Very few Roman clothes or shoes survive today. Fabric and leather are quick to rot. But we know how the Romans dressed from surviving paintings and statues.

Roman clothes showed whether a person was rich or poor, slave or Roman citizen. Most people, including children, wore simple tunics made of wool or linen. Wealthy women wore a long dress over the top called a *stola*. Their husbands could wear a *toga* if they were Roman citizens. Wool clothes or shawls kept people warm in cold weather.

HOW TO TIE YOUR TOGA
The toga (**A**) was a semicircle of cloth. To put it on, a man would drape one corner over his left shoulder until it reached his foot (**B**). He passed the other end under his right arm and across his left shoulder (**C**). It then had to be pinned and tucked to hold it in place.

_The slave wears a tunic,
while his master wears
a toga and his mistress a stola._

JEWELRY

Archaeologists have dug up many
pieces of Roman jewelry. Earrings
made from metal and precious
stones were very popular. Women
often had matching necklaces.
Men and women used brooches
to hold their clothes together.
Many people wore rings.

HAIRSTYLES

Many women wore elaborate
hairstyles held in place with
pins. Some dyed
their hair, while
others wore wigs.

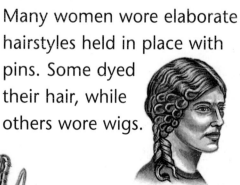

15

KEEPING CLEAN

Few Romans had a bath at home, so they visited the public bathhouse (the baths). A slave rubbed olive oil onto the bather's skin. In the heat of the baths, the bather sweated. The slave scraped the oil, sweat, and dirt off the skin by using a *strigil* (*right*).

Strigil

Oil flask

AT THE BATHS

The baths were cheap to use and free for children. On entering, Romans undressed and stored their clothes in a locker. They spent some time in warm or hot and steamy rooms, chatting with their friends. After a massage and a scraping, they took a dip in a cold pool. Clean at last!

1. *Undressing room*
2. *Hot, steamy room with hot bath*
3. *Cold dip bath*
4. *Exercise yard*
5. *Open pool*

HEATING THE BATHS

A large number of slaves worked at the baths to look after the fire that heated the baths. The fire blasted hot air under the raised floors and behind the walls of the baths. The nearer to the fire, the hotter the room.

Men and women visited the baths at different times of day. The man at the front of this picture is having his skin scraped clean with a strigil.

MYSTERY OBJECT

This little object is made of bronze. Each tool helped people get clean. Can you guess what it is?
(Answer on page 32.)

RELAXING

The Romans played sports, like catching games, in the exercise yard of the baths. They also enjoyed board games, using glass counters. Gambling with dice was another favorite pastime. Others enjoyed chatting or eating snacks with friends.

Dice

Glass counters

Ivory counter

17

GOING SHOPPING

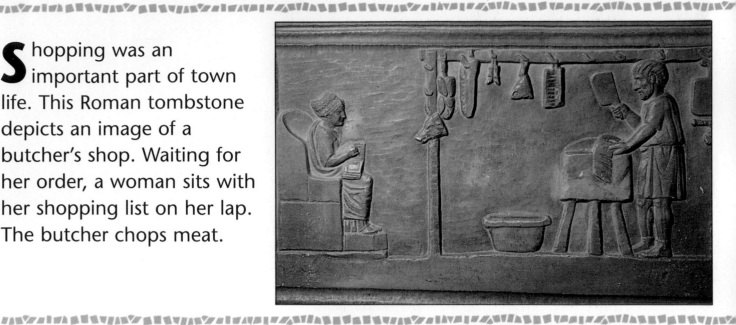

Shopping was an important part of town life. This Roman tombstone depicts an image of a butcher's shop. Waiting for her order, a woman sits with her shopping list on her lap. The butcher chops meat.

ROMAN SHOPS

Early in the morning, Roman shopkeepers removed the shutters from their shops. The shops were now open to the street and open for business.

Most Roman shops produced their goods for sale in the shop. If you went to buy bread, for instance, you would see the baker grinding the flour, kneading the dough, and baking the bread in the oven.

Romans used money to buy goods, just as we do today. The emperor's head was depicted on one side of the coin.

Some shops had signs advertising their goods. This illustration shows a clothmaker's sign that can still be seen above a doorway in Pompeii, Italy. The small pictures at the bottom show wool being cleaned, woven into cloth, and sold.

A busy Roman shopping street.

SOME OF THE GOODS FOR SALE ON A ROMAN SHOPPING STREET

Comb and mirror

Swan

Pillow

Fancy glassware and pottery

GOING SHOPPING

Roman towns had no supermarkets. Shoppers had to move from shop to shop, gathering up what they needed. Many shopkeepers and craftspeople lived in rooms behind or above their shops.

Farmers sold fresh food in open-air markets. In addition, sellers sold goods, such as sausages, from trays carried on their heads.

READING AND WRITING

Only the children of wealthier families learned to read and write. They used a reusable writing tablet (*right*). It had a thick layer of wax inside the wooden frame. The Romans used a pointed object, called a stylus, to scratch letters in the wax. The flat end smoothed the wax over to be used again.

WRITING MATERIALS

Wax tablets were not the only writing material. The Romans also wrote in pen and ink on thin layers of wood or papyrus, a type of paper made from reeds. The most expensive writing material was vellum, a thin layer of animal skin.

This clock uses Roman numerals, rather than our number system. I = 1, V= 5, and X = 10.

A	B	C	D	E
F	G	H	I	L
M	N	O	P	Q
R	S	T	V	X

THE ROMAN ALPHABET IS SHOWN ABOVE.
TRY USING IT TO WRITE A SENTENCE LIKE THE ONE BELOW.

READ ALL ABOUT THE ROMANS

CAN YOU READ WHAT IT SAYS?

School was usually a room in the teacher's house or a rented room in the town.

SCHOOL

Education in Roman times was not free. The sons, and a few of the daughters, of wealthier families started school at the age of seven. They learned some math and how to read and write Latin. At the age of 11, pupils went to secondary school and studied literature, history, math, and astronomy.

WRITERS

Homer (born ca. 725 BC) wrote two long poems in Greek—the _Iliad_ and the _Odyssey_ that were studied in Roman times.
Virgil (born 70 BC) wrote the _Aeneid_, among other poems.
Cicero (born 106 BC) was a Roman politician. Pupils studied his speeches.
Julius Caesar (born 100 BC) wrote accounts of his military campaigns.
Seneca (born ca. 4 BC) wrote many books about how Romans should live their lives.

| Homer | Virgil | Cicero | Julius Caesar | Seneca |

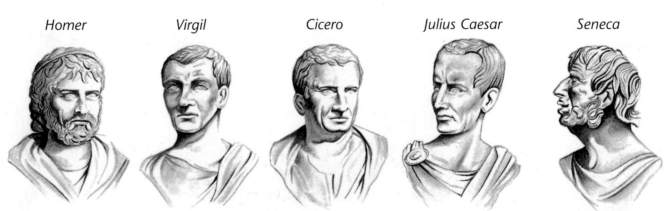

MAKING JOURNEYS

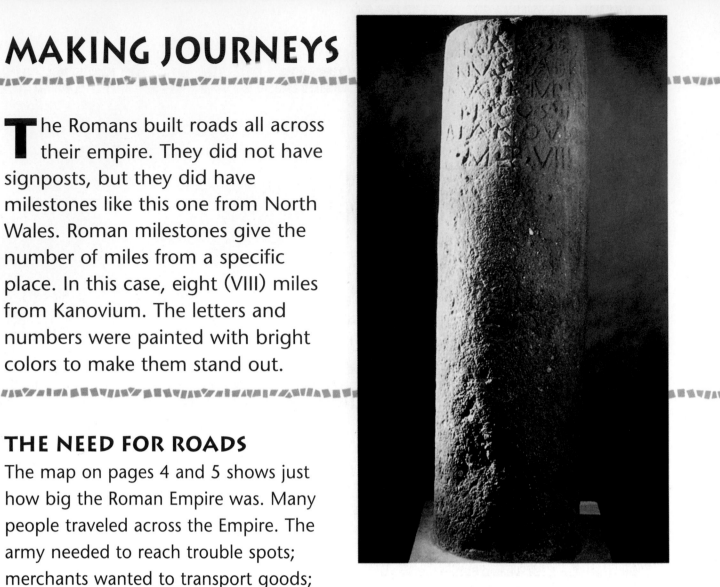

The Romans built roads all across their empire. They did not have signposts, but they did have milestones like this one from North Wales. Roman milestones give the number of miles from a specific place. In this case, eight (VIII) miles from Kanovium. The letters and numbers were painted with bright colors to make them stand out.

THE NEED FOR ROADS

The map on pages 4 and 5 shows just how big the Roman Empire was. Many people traveled across the Empire. The army needed to reach trouble spots; merchants wanted to transport goods; and government officials needed to travel to keep control of the empire.

When the Romans invaded new lands, their army built roads. After that, it was up to the local government to keep the roads in good repair and to build new ones.

The Romans built their roads so well that many survive today.

A horse-drawn stagecoach was the normal way to travel about the country. A traveler could expect to cover only 5 miles (8 km) a day.

COVERING LONG DISTANCES

Traveling by road was a dirty business. In summer, it was bumpy and dusty. In winter, it was wet and muddy. People could travel in stagecoaches. Some passengers sat inside; others sat on top.

Ships were used mainly to carry goods and could travel up to 100 miles (160 kilometers) a day. Many Romans wrote of their dislike of sea travel but had little choice for long journeys.

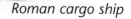

Transporting wine   *Carrying supplies*   *Cart for farm produce*   *Roman cargo ship*

GOING TO A SHOW

Romans who lived in towns could choose from a variety of shows for their entertainment. This decorated pot (*right*) shows a gladiator fight, which was a popular show. The gladiators' names are written above them—Memnon (*left*) and Valentinus (*right*). Valentinus is holding up one finger as a sign that he is asking for mercy from Memnon.

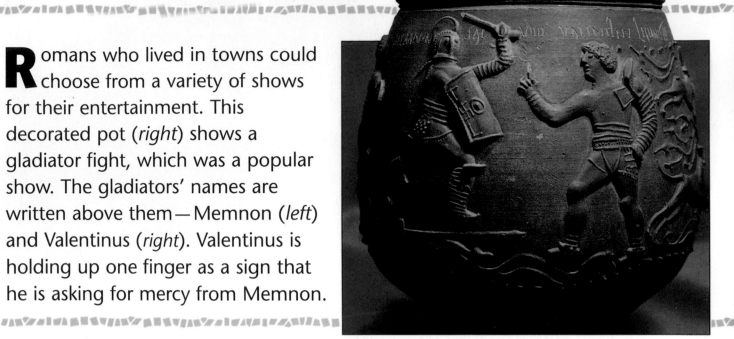

GREAT STADIUMS

The Romans built grand buildings for entertainment. Wealthy Roman politicians and leaders paid for many of the shows to gain public support. Thousands attended—perhaps 20,000 to watch a play, 50,000 to watch gladiator fights, and 200,000 to watch chariot races.

CHARIOTEERS

At the races, charioteers drove chariots pulled by four horses. Competing in teams, each one was represented by a different color—the Reds, the Blues, the Greens, and the Whites. Skilled charioteers became wealthy, but it was a dangerous sport with many deaths.

Gladiators usually fought to the death. Sometimes, the audience spared the life of the loser.

A Roman mosaic shows actors preparing for a performance.

MUSIC AND THEATER

The Romans had plenty of opportunities to watch plays at the theater. The actors wore face masks to help their voices reach to the back of the huge, open-air, theaters. The type of mask and the costume helped the audience understand the story. While musicians performed music as part of the play, they also gave concerts in small theaters called *odeons*.

IN THE ARMY

The Romans had one of the greatest armies that has ever existed. Their soldiers were well trained and well armed. This iron and bronze helmet (*right*) was worn by a cavalryman—a soldier on horseback. The helmets worn by foot soldiers, called legionaries, were very similar.

FIGHTING WEAPONS

The helmet was only part of the soldier's equipment for battle. He also wore body armor or chain mail. The soldier's main weapon was a short sword (*below*), but he also carried a dagger and spears.

The shield weighed about 13 pounds (6 kg) and was decorated with metal strips and paint.

The iron sword, inside its scabbard, was carried on the soldier's right side.

A legionary soldier's body armor was made of iron plates. Hinged to fit the body, it allowed the soldier to move and fight.

Each legionary soldier carried two spears for battle. The long iron tip was fixed onto a wooden shaft.

Daggers were often decorated and were about 10 inches (25 cm) long.

Guards kept watch at the fort's four gates and from the watch towers.

SOLDIERS OF RANK

As in any army, Roman soldiers were of different rank and held particular jobs.

Legionary Cavalryman Standard bearer

Centurian Auxiliary

THE FORT

All over the empire, the Romans built forts to house the army. Inside each fort, the soldiers lived in long buildings divided into at least ten pairs of rooms. Each pair of rooms housed eight men. One room had bunkbeds while the other room was for cooking and storing equipment. When the soldiers were on the move, they made camps at night and slept in tents.

BUILDERS AND ENGINEERS

The Romans were skilled builders and engineers. Many of their buildings survive today. The Pont du Gard (*right*) carried an aqueduct (water channel). It ran for more than 31 miles (50 km) and carried 20,000 tons (20,000 t) of water a day to the people of Nîmes, France.

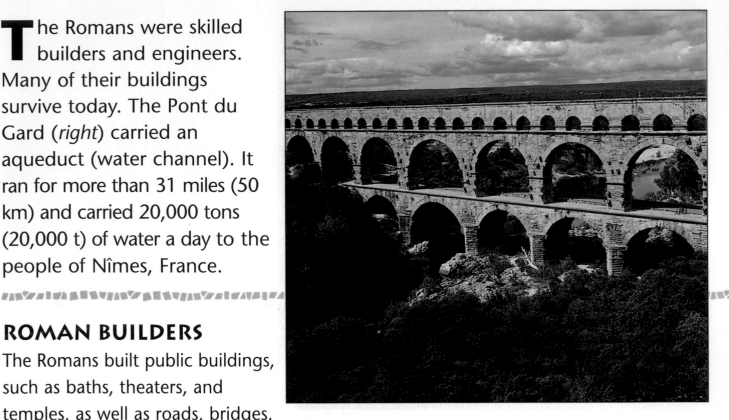

ROMAN BUILDERS

The Romans built public buildings, such as baths, theaters, and temples, as well as roads, bridges, and blocks of apartments. The Romans discovered how to make concrete out of volcanic rocks and rubble. This allowed them to build even bigger buildings as concrete is not as heavy as stone.

THE GROMA

The groma (*below*) was used by a surveyor to mark out straight lines in building projects. Using the groma, the Romans built extremely straight roads.

The weights hanging down from the groma held the strings straight.

A Roman crane lifts
blocks of stone for the bridge.

BUILDING THE BRIDGE

During the reign of Emperor Claudius
(27 BC–AD 14) the Pont du Gard was
built to carry the aqueduct across a river.
Roman engineers had a variety of tools
and machines to help them, including a
crane. People powered the crane by
walking inside the wheel. It lifted heavy
blocks of stone, cut to the right size
by skilled workers.

Many streets had fountains and water troughs,
which were filled by underground pipes. People
fetched water for use at home.

WORSHIPPING THE GODS

Religion was an important part of life and death. This Roman tombstone shows the funeral feast of Julia Velva, who lies surrounded by her family. The Romans believed it was extremely important to mourn people properly in order to send them on their journey to the afterlife, which they called Hades.

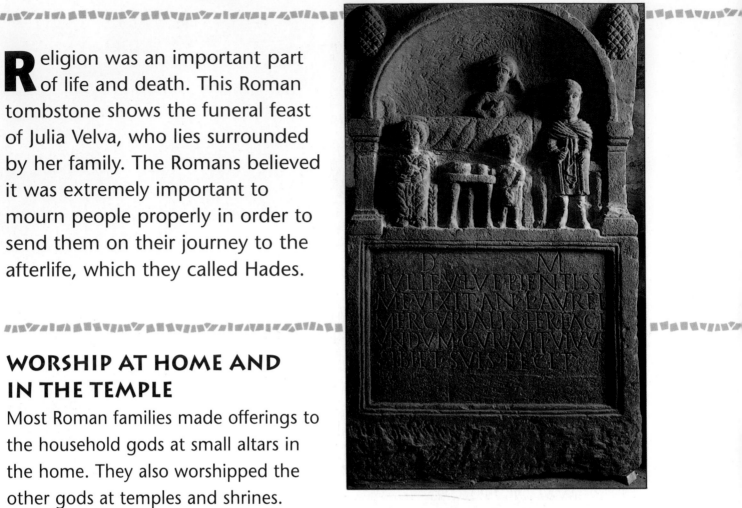

WORSHIP AT HOME AND IN THE TEMPLE

Most Roman families made offerings to the household gods at small altars in the home. They also worshipped the other gods at temples and shrines.

Household altar

GODS AND GODDESSES

For most of the Roman period, the Romans worshipped a large number of gods and goddesses. People believed that each god or goddess could help them in a different way. Toward the end of the Roman Empire, Christianity became the official religion.

Minerva was the goddess of wisdom, crafts, trades, and industry. She is often shown in armor.

Some families paid actors and musicians to lead the funeral processions of their loved one.

FUNERALS

At different times in the Roman period, people were either cremated or buried. After an elaborate funeral, people carried the ashes or body to the cemetery, just outside the town walls and along the roadside.

Jupiter was the god of the sky and king of all the gods. He was called "the greatest and the best."

Apollo was a Greek god worshipped by the Romans. They believed he could reveal the future.

Mithras was originally a Persian god. Soldiers and merchants particularly liked his bravery.

Neptune was the god of water and the sea. He is usually shown with a pronged spear.

INDEX

ANSWERS TO MYSTERY OBJECT BOXES

Page 8: This farm machine is called a *vallus*. The donkey pushed the machine, with its rotating blades, into the crop. The blades cut the corn, which fell into the scoop.

Page 17: This is a personal grooming set. The top tool was used to scoop out ear wax. The middle one was used to clean nails. The last one is a pair of tweezers to remove splinters.